Introduction

atisfying, quick and simple to prepare,
ancakes are a welcome treat at any
ne of the year whether you're cooking
r two, throwing a party or planning a
idweek meal for the family.

ontinental-style pancakes, such as
pain's tortilla and Switzerland's rosti are
enerally served flat, as are some of the
ther potato-based pancakes in the
ook.

good, heavy-based frying pan, pref-
rably non-stick is a good investment for
ooking successful pancakes.

All spoon r
15ml spoo

Follow EITH
NEVER mix
changeab

Eggs used a.. a medium size 3 unless otherwise
stated.

For additional hints and tips on preparing and
cooking pancakes, and clarifying butter, see
step-by-step instructions and pictures on pages
18-19 and 34-35. Clarified butter gives best results
in these recipes but if preferred, use melted,
unsalted butter.

Kilojoules and kilocalories at the end of each
recipe are represented by the letters kj and kcal.

Written by Elisabeth Döpp

Apple Pancakes

Serves 2

A substantial and healthy pancake.

Preparation time: about 30 minutes
Standing time: 30 minutes
Cooking time: about 25 minutes

PANCAKE BATTER
60g (2oz) plain flour
Pinch of salt
2 eggs, beaten
155ml (5 fl oz/⅔ cup) cold milk
2tsp clarified (concentrated) butter, melted

TOPPING
2 cooking apples
½ tsp cinnamon
½ tsp caster sugar
1tsp lemon juice
5tsp clarified (concentrated) butter, melted
    and cooled

1 To make batter, sift flour and salt into mixing bowl. Add eggs, milk and butter and beat to smooth batter. Cover and chill for 30 minutes.

2 Meanwhile prepare topping. Peel, quarter, core and slice apples. Simmer gently in covered pan with cinnamon, sugar, lemon juice and 2tsp butter for about 20 minutes.

3 Stir batter and if it appears too thick after standing, beat in 1tbsp warm water.

4 Melt half remaining butter in 20cm (8in) heavy-based, non-stick frying pan until hot.

5 Add half the stewed apple. Top with half the batter mixture and spread smoothly over apples. Fry for 3 minutes. Turn pancake over following instructions and step-by-step pictures on pages 34-35. Fry second side of pancake for about 2 minutes or until golden brown underneath.

6 Turn pancake out on to warm plate and keep hot. Heat remaining butter in pan and fry second pancake in same way. Serve pancakes as they are or sprinkle with extra sugar and cinnamon. Alternatively, serve with whipped cream sweetened with honey, or scoops of vanilla ice cream.

Nutritional value per portion:
about 1700kj/400kcal
Protein: 12g
Fat: 22g
Carbohydrate: 40g

Apple Pancakes

Meat and Pineapple-Filled Pancakes

Serves 3

A substantial main meal which goes well with a crisp green salad.

Preparation time: about 40 minutes
Standing time: 1 hour
Cooking time: about 1 hour

SOUFFLE PANCAKE BATTER

100g (3½ oz) plain flour
1/2tsp salt
155ml (5fl oz/⅔ cup) milk
90ml (3fl oz/⅓ cup) sparkling mineral water
1 egg, separated
1tbsp sunflower or corn oil
green salad for serving

FILLING

4 medium tomatoes
1 small onion
1 clove garlic
155g (5oz) fresh or canned pineapple
2tsp sunflower or corn oil
125g (4oz) lean minced beef
½tsp salt
Freshly milled black pepper to taste
1tbsp finely chopped fresh parsley
Pinch of sugar
2tsp margarine
Pinch of paprika

1 To make batter, sift flour and salt into bowl. Gradually beat in milk, mineral water, egg yolk and 1tsp oil until smooth. Cover and chill for 1 hour.

2 Meanwhile, prepare filling. Cover tomatoes with boiling water for 30 seconds, then plunge into cold water and peel away skins. Cut tomatoes in half, remove any pieces of hard core and chop. Peel onion and garlic and chop both finely. Peel pineapple if fresh, or drain well, if canned. Cut pineapple into small pieces.

3 Heat oil in pan until hot, but not smoking. Add onion and garlic and sauté until pale golden. Stir in meat and stir-fry until brown and crumbly. Add tomatoes.

4 Season with salt and pepper, cover and simmer over low heat for 20 minutes. Stir in parsley and sugar. Melt margarine and sauté pineapple separately for 3 minutes. Season with paprika. Stir into meat mixture.

5 To complete pancakes, whisk egg whites until stiff then fold into batter mixture with large metal spoon.

6 Heat a little oil in 15cm (6in) heavy-based, non-stick frying pan. Spoon in enough batter to cover base of pan and fry for 1½-2 minutes until underside is golden. Turn over with fish slice and cook until golden.

7 Put pancake on to plate set over pan of gently boiling water to keep warm. Repeat process to make 5 more pancakes.

8 Fill each pancake with meat mixture, roll up and serve straight away with salad.

Nutritional value per portion:
about 2300kj/550kcal
Protein: 28g
Fat: 23g
Carbohydrate: 55g

Meat and Pineapple-Filled Pancakes

Italian Potato Pancakes

Serves 2

A real winner for lunch or supper with a topping of Bolognese sauce, grilled tomato slices o fried mushrooms.

Preparation time: about 20 minutes
Cooking time: about 40 minutes

2 large cold cooked jacket potatoes
4 eggs
1tsp salt
White pepper to taste
1 clove garlic
4tsp clarified (concentrated) butter
Sage leaves for garnishing
Mixed salad for serving

1 Peel potatoes and grate coarsely.

2 Break eggs into bowl and beat until foamy. Season with salt and pepper.

3 Peel and crush garlic and add to eggs with grated potatoes.

4 Melt half the butter in 20cm (8in) heavy-based, non-stick frying pan. When hot but not smoking, add half egg and potato mixture and fry for 2-3 minutes until underside is golden.

5 Turn over pancake following instructions and step-by-step pictures on pages 34-35. Alternatively, hold pan under hot grill until top is set or cover pan with lid and leave over low heat for 2 minutes. The top will set but will remain pale in colour.

6 Slide out pancake on to warm plate, garnish with sage and keep hot. Melt remaining butter in pan and fry second pancake in same way. Serve with salad.

TIP
Make two pancakes following recipe, leave to become completely cold then cut into small portions and serve as a cocktail snack with pesto or olive pâté.

Nutritional value per portion:
about 1100kj/260kcal
Protein: 7g
Fat: 10g
Carbohydrate: 35g

Italian Potato Pancakes

Pancakes with Smoked Fish

Serves 3

These pancakes are low in fat and are ideal for those watching their cholesterol intake.

Preparation time: about 20 minutes
Standing time: 1 hour
Cooking time: about 20 minutes

SOUFFLE PANCAKE BATTER
125g (4oz) plain flour
½ tsp salt
250ml (8fl oz/1 cup) sparkling mineral water
1 egg, separated
4tsp sunflower or corn oil

TO SERVE
2 smoked trout or smoked mackerel fillets
Lemon juice
½ medium cucumber
3tbsp thick Greek-style yogurt
Sprigs of fresh dill
Salt and pepper to taste

1 Sift flour and salt into mixing bowl. Add mineral water, egg and oil and gradually beat to smooth batter. Cover and chill for 1 hour.

2 Skin fish fillets if necessary, taking care not to break up flesh. Cut fish fillets carefully in half lengthwise and cut in half again. Sprinkle with lemon juice.

3 Peel cucumber, cut in half lengthwise, remove seeds and thinly slice.

4 Tip yogurt into small bowl. Wash and dry half the dill and chop finely. Add to yogurt and season with salt and pepper

5 To complete pancakes, whisk egg whites until stiff then gently fold into batter mixture until well combined.

6 Heat a little oil in a 20cm (8in) non-stick frying pan. Pour in one sixth of batter and spread evenly over base of pan.

7 Fry for 2 minutes until underside is golden. Turn over following instructions and step-by-step pictures on pages 34-35. Repeat process to make 5 more pancakes.

8 Fold each pancake in half, transfer to 3 warm serving plates and serve straight away with fish, cucumber and sauce and garnished with remaining dill sprigs.

Nutritional value per portion:
about 1800kj/430kcal
Protein: 31g
Fat: 14g
Carbohydrate: 44g

Pancakes with Smoked Fish

Spanish Tortilla

Serves 2

Spain's imaginative answer to pancakes, the tortilla is basically an omelette filled with potatoes, tomatoes and peppers (capsicums).

Preparation time: about 20 minutes
Cooking time: about 25 minutes

2 medium onions
1 large peeled boiled potato
2 medium tomatoes
½ small red pepper (capsicum)
30g (1oz) butter or margarine
4 eggs
2tsp cold water
½ tsp salt
White pepper to taste
Green salad for serving

1 Peel and slice onions. Separate slices into rings. Cut potatoes into small cubes. Cover tomatoes with boiling water for 30 seconds, then plunge into cold water and peel away skins. Cut tomatoes in half, remove any pieces of hard core and chop, discarding seeds. Remove inner white membranes and seeds from pepper (capsicum) and finely chop flesh.

2 Melt butter or margarine in 25cm (10in) non-stick frying pan. Add onion rings and potatoes and sauté over moderate heat until light golden. Add tomatoes and pepper (capsicum) and stir-fry for 10 minutes over low heat.

3 Beat eggs and water until frothy and season with salt and pepper. Pour into pan over vegetables.

4 Cook pancake gently until base is firm, golden and crispy. Preheat grill.

5 Holding pan by its handle, stand pan under hot grill for about 2 minutes to set top. Alternatively, cover with lid and leave over low heat for 2 minutes. The top will set but will stay pale golden in colour.

6 Slide out pancake on to warm plate, cut into 2 portions and serve warm with salad.

Nurtitional value per portion:
about 930kJ/220kcal
Protein: 10g
Fat: 15g
Carbohydrate: 13g

Spanish Tortilla

Potato and Herb Pancakes with Fried Pork

Serves 2

A satisfying main course dish from Germany.

Preparation time: about 30 minutes
Cooking time: 20 minutes

155g (5oz) pork fillet
2tsp sunflower or corn oil
Salt and pepper to taste
60ml (2fl oz/¼ cup) dry white wine
1tbsp crème fraîche

POTATO PANCAKES

375g (12oz) floury potatoes
1 small onion
5tsp plain flour
1 egg, beaten
4tsp finely chopped fresh parsley
¼tsp freshly grated nutmeg
1tsp salt
3tsp sunflower or corn oil
Orange slices, cranberry sauce and sprigs of fresh parsley for garnishing

1 Cube meat and wipe with absorbent kitchen paper.

2 Heat oil in frying pan, add pork and stir-fry fairly briskly for 6 minutes until well-browned on all sides. Remove to plate lined with absorbent kitchen paper and sprinkle with salt and pepper to taste. Keep hot.

3 Add wine to juices left in pan and cook, uncovered, until reduced by half. Stir in crème fraîche and return pork to pan. Keep hot.

4 To make pancakes, peel and wash potatoes. Peel onion. Grate both into mixing bowl and stir in flour, beaten egg, parsley, nutmeg and salt.

5 Heat half the oil in 25cm (10in) non-stick frying pan. Add half the potato pancake mixture and spread smoothly over base of pan.

6 Fry pancake for 5 minutes. Turn over following instructions and step-by-step pictures on pages 34-35. When second side is golden, slide on to warm plate and keep hot. Using remaining oil, make second pancake in same way.

7 Top pancakes with fried pork and sauce. Garnish with orange slices, cranberry sauce and parsley.

Nutritional value per portion:
about 2500kj/600kcal
Protein: 25g
Fat: 28g
Carbohydrate: 60g

Potato and Herb Pancakes with Fried Pork

Leek and Bacon Pancakes

Serves 3

Perfect for a hearty winter's lunch.

Preparation time: about 1 hour
Standing time: 1 hour

SOUFFLE PANCAKE BATTER
170g (5½ oz) plain flour
1/2tsp salt
125ml (4fl oz/½ cup) milk
90ml (3fl oz/⅓ cup) sparkling mineral water
2 eggs, separated
Sunflower or corn oil for frying

FILLING
3 medium leeks
125ml (4fl oz/½ cup) boiling salted water
15g (½ oz) butter or margarine
3tsp finely chopped fresh parsley
Salt and pepper
125g(4oz) streaky bacon, rind removed
3tsp snipped fresh chives

1 To make pancake batter, sift flour and salt into mixing bowl. Gradually add milk, mineral water and egg yolks and beat until mixture is smooth. Cover and chill for 1 hour.

2 Meanwhile prepare filling. Top and tail leeks then slit each one lengthwise. Wash thoroughly under cold running water to remove earth and grit between leaves and shake dry. Cut diagonally into thin slices.

3 Cook leeks in the boiling salted water for 12 minutes. Drain and reserve cooking liquor.

4 Melt butter or margarine in saucepan. Add reserved leek liquor and parsley. Boil, uncovered, until reduced by two-thirds. Add leeks, season to taste with salt and pepper and keep hot.

5 Cut bacon into small pieces and fry, without additional fat, until light golden.

6 To complete pancakes, whisk egg whites until stiff. Stir chives and bacon into batter mixture then gently fold in egg whites until well combined.

7 Heat a little oil in an 18cm (7in) non-stick frying pan. Pour in one sixth of pancake batter and spread over base of pan with back of spoon. Fry for 2 minutes until underside is golden. Turn over with fish slice and fry second side for 2-3 minutes until golden brown.

8 Repeat process to make 5 more pancakes. Fill with leek mixture and roll up. Serve straight away.

Nutritional value per portion:
about 2200kj/520kcal
Protein: 24g
Fat: 20g
Carbohydrate: 62g

Leek and Bacon Pancakes

Step-by-step

BASIC PANCAKE BATTER

1 Sift flour and salt into bowl. Using hand-held whisk or electric beaters, gradually beat in liquid (milk and/or water).

2 Break up egg with fork and beat into batter until smooth.

3 Beat in 1tsp sunflower or corn oil to batter to prevent pancakes from sticking to pan during cooking. Cover and chill for 1 hour before using.

SOUFFLÉ PANCAKE BATTER

4 Sift flour and salt into mixing bowl. Gradually beat in mineral water followed by egg yolk(s). Cover and chill for 1 hour.

5 Beat batter using hand-held whisk or electric beaters until completely smooth.

6 Whisk egg whites until stiff and fold gradually into batter with large metal spoon or balloon whisk. DO NOT USE electric beaters or batter will lose its lightness.

RUSSIAN POTATO PANCAKES

7 Cut peeled, raw potatoes into large pieces. Grate potato and onion into sieve placed over mixing bowl and drain for 5 minutes. Pour off water and put grated potatoes into clean bowl.

8 Grate in cooked potato and add flour, eggs, salt and pepper.

9 Combine raw and cooked potatoes and use as directed in recipes.

1

4

7

3

6

9

19

Russian Potato Pancakes with Smoked Salmon

Serves 4

Serve these pancakes with thick sour cream.

Preparation time: about 25 minutes
Standing time: 30 minutes
Cooking time: about 20 minutes

750g (1 ½ lb) floury potatoes
1 medium onion
1 medium cooked potato
6tsp plain flour
2 eggs, beaten
1½ tsp salt
Freshly milled white pepper to taste
Sunflower or corn oil for frying
Fresh dill for garnishing
185g (6oz) smoked salmon rolls for serving

1 Peel, wash and grate raw potatoes and onion directly into mixing bowl. Grate in cooked potato.

2 Stir in flour, eggs, salt and pepper to taste. Mix thoroughly, cover and leave to stand at room temperature for 30 minutes. The potatoes will discolour during this time.

3 Heat about 5cm (1in) oil in large heavy-based, non-stick frying pan. When hot, but not smoking, add 3-4 tablespoons of potato pancake mixture.

4 Flatten pancakes with back of spoon and fry for 3 minutes. Turn over and fry second side for 2 minutes. Repeat process with remaining batter.

5 Drain pancakes on absorbent kitchen paper. Put on to 4 warm serving plates, garnish with dill and serve with smoked salmon.

Nutritional value per portion:
about 1700kj/400kcal
Protein: 21g
Fat: 17g
Carbohydrate: 46g

Russian Potato Pancakes with Smoked Salmon

Turkey and Vegetable Pancakes

Serves 4

Pancakes topped with a strips of turkey and a colourful selection of vegetables.

Preparation time: about 30 minutes
Standing time: 1 hour
Cooking time: about 45 minutes

BASIC PANCAKE BATTER
125g (4oz) plain flour
Pinch of salt
315ml (10fl oz/1¼ cups) cold milk
2 eggs, beaten
1tsp sunflower or corn oil, plus extra for frying

TOPPING
4 medium courgettes (zucchini)
4 medium tomatoes
2 medium onions
2 cloves garlic
315g (10oz) turkey breast fillet
3tsp sunflower or corn oil
125ml (4fl oz/½ cup) white wine
Salt and pepper to taste

1 To make batter, sift flour and salt into bowl. Gradually whisk in milk and beaten eggs. Continue to beat until batter is smooth and creamy in consistency. Add oil. Cover and chill for 1 hour. Stir before using.

2 Meanwhile prepare topping. Top and tail courgettes (zucchini) and thinly slice. Cover tomatoes with boiling water for 30 seconds, then plunge into cold water and peel away skins. Cut tomatoes in half, remove any pieces of hard core and coarsely chop. Peel onions and garlic and finely chop. Cut turkey into 1cm (½ in) strips.

3 Heat oil in saucepan until hot. Add onions, garlic and turkey and sauté briskly until light golden brown. Add courgettes (zucchini) and stir-fry for 4 minutes. Stir in tomatoes and wine and season with salt and pepper.

4 Bring to boil, stirring continuously. Half-cover pan with lid and simmer mixture gently for 20 minutes until turkey is tender and about half the liquid has evaporated.

5 Make 8 pancakes from batter following instructions and step-by-step pictures on pages 34-35 using a 20cm (8in) non-stick frying pan and brushing pan lightly with oil after each pancake is cooked.

6 Put pancakes on to 4 warm plates and top with turkey mixture. Serve straight away.

Nutritional value per portion:
about 1600kj/380kcal
Protein: 30g
Fat: 14g
Carbohydrate: 33g

Turkey and Vegetable Pancakes

Yogurt Pancakes with Oranges and Ice Cream

Serves 4

Refreshing ginger and orange pancakes served with orange segments and mint.

Preparation time: about 25 minutes
Standing time: 1 hour
Cooking time: about 20 minutes

BASIC PANCAKE BATTER

125g (4oz) plain flour
½ tsp ground ginger
¼ tsp salt
315ml (10fl oz/1 1/4 cups) cold milk
2 eggs, well beaten
1tsp sunflower or corn oil
1tsp finely grated orange rind
Extra sunflower or corn oil for frying

TO SERVE

2 medium oranges
Maple syrup
Ice cream
Sprigs of fresh mint

1 To make batter, sift flour, ginger and salt into mixing bowl. Gradually whisk in milk and beaten eggs. Stir in oil and orange rind. Cover and chill for 1 hour. Stir before using.

2 Make 8 pancakes following instructions and step-by-step pictures on pages 34-35, using a 20cm (8in) non-stick frying pan and brushing pan lightly with oil after each pancake is cooked.

3 Keep pancakes hot on plate set over saucepan of gently boiling water, separating each pancake with a square of greaseproof paper.

4 Before serving, peel oranges and remove pith. Cut out segments of flesh between fibrous skin with sharp knife, working over bowl to catch juice.

5 Stir maple syrup into orange juice. Fold each pancake in half, then in half again. Put pancakes on to 4 warm serving plates. Spoon over orange juice mixture and serve with orange segments, ice cream and mint leaves.

Nutritional value per portion:
about 2100kj/500kcal
Protein: 10g
Fat: 23g
Carbohydrate: 62g

Yogurt Pancakes with Oranges and Ice Cream

Cinnamon Pancakes & Raspberry Sauce

Serves 4

Made with self-raising flour, these pancakes are light and fluffy and are served with an aromatic raspberry sauce.

Preparation time: about 30 minutes
Standing time: 1 hour
Cooking time: about 20 minutes

SAUCE
250g (8oz) fresh or frozen raspberries
90ml (3fl oz/⅓ cup) sparkling white wine
3tsp clear honey
3 fresh mint leaves, finely chopped
Sprigs of fresh mint and whole raspberries for garnishing

BASIC PANCAKE BATTER
125g (4oz) self-raising flour
¼ tsp salt
250ml (8fl oz/1 cup) cold milk
3 eggs, separated
1tsp sunflower or corn oil, plus extra for frying

1 For sauce. Gently wash fresh raspberries. Bring wine and honey to boil in saucepan. Add half the raspberries and chopped mint. Return to boil, stirring. Remove pan from heat.

2 Purée fruit by rubbing through fine sieve or blending smoothly in food processor or blender. Tip into bowl and stir in remaining raspberries. Keep warm.

3 To make batter, sift flour and salt into mixing bowl. Gradually whisk in milk and egg yolks until smooth and creamy. Cover and chill for 15 minutes.

4 Whisk egg whites until stiff and gently fold into batter with large metal spoon.

5 Make 8 pancakes following instructions and step-by-step pictures on pages 34-35, using a 20cm (8in) non-stick frying pan and brushing pan lightly with oil after each pancake is cooked. Keep pancakes hot on plate set over pan of gently boiling water, separating each pancake with square of greaseproof paper.

6 Put pancakes on to 4 warm serving plates. Top with raspberry sauce and fold in half. Decorate with mint and whole raspberries.

Nutritional value per portion:
about 2200kj/520kcal
Protein: 8g
Fat: 34g
Carbohydrate: 47g

Cinnamon Pancakes & Raspberry Sauce

Mango Pancakes

Serves 4

Oriental in character and easily made with canned mangoes.

Preparation time: about 25 minutes
Standing time: 15 minutes
Cooking time: about 20 minutes

MANGO MIXTURE
425g (15oz) canned mangoes in syrup
2.5cm (1in) piece cinnamon stick
2tsp rosewater
Seeds from 1 green cardamom pod
4 tsp icing sugar for decorating

BASIC PANCAKE BATTER
125g (4oz) self-raising flour
Pinch of salt
½ tsp garam masala
1tsp caster sugar
250ml (8fl oz/1 cup) milk
3 eggs, separated
Sunflower or corn oil for frying

1 Drain mangoes thoroughly and cut fruit into small cubes. Put into saucepan with 3tbsp mango syrup from can, cinnamon stick, rosewater and cardamom seeds. Reserve remaining syrup for fruit salads or drinks.

2 Simmer gently, uncovered, for 5 minutes. Remove pan from heat and drain, reserving syrup and mangoes in 2 separate bowls. Discard cinnamon stick.

3 To make batter, sift flour, salt, garam masala and sugar into mixing bowl. Gradually whisk in milk and egg yolks until smooth and creamy. Cover and chill for 15 minutes.

4 Whisk egg whites until stiff. Gently fold egg whites into batter with large metal spoon. Stir in chopped mango.

5 Make 8 pancakes following instructions and step-by-step pictures on pages 34-35, using a 20cm (8in) non-stick frying pan and brushing pan lightly with oil after each pancake is cooked.

6 Put pancakes on to 4 warm serving plates and moisten with syrup in which mangoes were simmered. Decorate with sifted icing sugar and serve warm.

Nutritional value per portion:
about 1500kj/360kcal
Protein: 13g
Fat: 15g
Carbohydrate: 45g

Mango Pancakes

Fruit Salad Pancakes

Serves 4

These pancakes are luxuriously filled with mixed fresh fruit and honey and served with ice cream.

Preparation time: about 30 minutes
Standing time: 15 minutes
Cooking time: about 20 minutes

BASIC PANCAKE MIXTURE
125g (4oz) self-raising flour
Pinch of salt
250ml (8fl oz/1 cup) milk
3 eggs, separated
Sunflower or corn oil for frying

FILLING
2 medium bananas
250g (8oz) strawberries
4tsp honey
4tsp lime juice
½ tsp vanilla essence
Vanilla ice cream, sliced strawberries and bananas for serving
Sprigs of fresh mint for decorating

1 To make batter, sift flour and salt into mixing bowl. Gradually whisk in milk and egg yolks until smooth and creamy. Cover and chill for 15 minutes.

2 Whisk egg whites until stiff then gently fold into batter with large metal spoon.

3 Make 8 pancakes following instructions and step-by-step pictures on pages 34-35, using a 20cm (8in) non-stick frying pan and brushing pan lightly with oil after each pancake is cooked.

4 Keep pancakes hot on a plate set over a pan of gently boiling water, separating each pancake with square of grease-proof paper.

5 To make filling, slice peeled bananas into saucepan. Add rinsed and sliced strawberries, honey, lime juice and vanilla essence. Heat gently for 5 minutes, then coarsely mash.

6 Put pancakes on to 4 warm serving plates. Spread equal amounts of filling over each and roll up. Add a scoop of vanilla ice cream to each and add extra sliced fruit to serve. Decorate with mint.

Nutritional value per portion:
about 2400kj/570kcal
Protein: 14g
Fat: 27g
Carbohydrate: 68g

Fruit Salad Pancakes

Emperor's Omelette

Serves 2

A classic from Austria, this is an omelette pancake which is torn into pieces while it cooks and fried until crispy. It goes perfectly with canned or stewed apricots or bottled morello cherries flavoured with Kirsch.

Preparation time: about 7 minutes
Cooking time: 20-30 minutes

60g (2oz) plain flour
Pinch of salt
30g (1oz) fine semolina
2 eggs, separated
155ml (5fl oz/⅔ cup) milk
1½ tbsp caster sugar
45g (1½ oz) clarified (concentrated) butter, melted
Fresh mint sprigs for decorating
Apricots or cherries for serving

1 Sift flour and salt into mixing bowl then add semolina.

2 Add egg yolks, milk and half the sugar and beat to smooth batter. Whisk egg whites until stiff then fold gently into batter with large metal spoon.

3 Melt butter in a 25cm (10in) heavy-based frying pan until hot, but not smoking. Add batter mixture and cook over moderate heat for about 5 minutes until underside is golden.

4 Using 2 forks or 2 spatulas if pan is non-stick, tear omelette into small pieces as it cooks.

5 Stir-fry each piece until golden brown and crisp. Put on to 2 warm serving plates and sprinkle with remaining sugar. Decorate with mint and serve hot with fruit.

Nutritional value per portion:
about 2575kj/615kcal
Protein: 27g
Fat: 14g
Carbohydrate: 95g

Emperor's Omelette

Step-by-step

HOW TO CLARIFY BUTTER

1 Melt required amount of butter in saucepan. Keep heat low to prevent it burning.

2 Carefully remove white foam from top of butter with absorbent kitchen paper. Remove pan from heat and set aside for 20 minutes so that any sediment has time to settle.

3 Pour butter slowly into clean container and use as required.

MAKING PANCAKES

1 Oil or butter a heavy-based frying pan and heat until hot. Add just enough batter to cover base. Twirl pan gently in all directions until batter flows to edges.

2 Ease edges away from pan with fork or spatula.

3 Gently slide pancake on to large warm plate.

4 Hold plate underneath with flat of your hand and using your other hand, place frying pan upside-down over plate.

5 Holding plate and pan firmly, quickly turn over, removing plate. Alternatively, toss in traditional way. Fry second side until golden and cooked.

6 Put cooked pancake on to plate and fill as directed in recipe.